Spring Surprises Silly & Serious

Spring Surprises Silly & Serious

Poems To See You Through Spring

Sandra Matthews

Sheephouse Books

Note From The Author

Thank your for reading my poetry book.
These books are called "Silly & Serious"
because they are based on real life which
comes in all shades.

Perhaps you may call me lazy but when I
read a poem I want it to speak to me
without my having to disect and study it too
much. There was enough of that in English
class in school. Now my poetry reading is
for pleasure, comfort, inspiration and a
giggle sometimes too.

I hope these poems speak to you wherever
you are.

And on with the writing I go.

Love Sandra

Thank you to my family and friends for all of your encouragment, support and editing

For my "Comfortable Friends".
You know who you are

Contents

Page No.

Contents

Brightness
&
New Growth

Seasons

She moved from Chicago

to live in L.A.

Told me she missed

the seasons

For now the weather

stayed the same

day after day after day

When I catch myself wishing

for days always clear

I can hear

her words again

For we can see the value dear

When something is

no longer here

Surprises

Spring surprises us
With glimpses of light
Clusters of daffodils
Daydreams fresh and new

Oh the things we will now do
With winter gone

Places we will visit
With bright days long

Stretching out of our cobwebs
We plan
Because we can

With hours of natural light
Fuelling our will to fight

For a life of vision and goals
Doing things that feed our souls
No longer trapped in pigeon holes

The real me
The real you

Doing things we were born to do
When Spring comes
With surprises new

Winter
By Another Name

Early Spring in Ireland
Winter by another name

Promise of change reassures us
While temperatures stay the same

Rain spits down upon us
Bitter, cold and sharp

Summer seems impossibly far
Clutching scarves tight
We dash to the car

Shivering, thawing
In out of the breeze

Rain falls to sleet
Roads race to freeze

Nothingness looms
Nothingness booms

Why call it Spring
While ice holds such sting?

Why build this season's
Claim to fame

When it is but winter
By another name

St Brigid's Day

St. Brigid's Day was Mam's birthday
A sentimental time each year

So too the remembered voice
Of my father in law I hear

St Brigid's Day is the first of Spring
We speak of hope while cold winds sting

Warm weather feels a world away
The first of February a bleak cold day

My father in law

He knew the land

When the Dublin girl

Could not understand

How Spring had sprung
Though nothing changed
No signs of seasons rearranged

He talked of growth beneath the ground
Stirrings of new life

With patience he explained such things
To his son's young wife

All I could see was cold
While growth was taking hold

Whispering first then shouting bold
Colours of green and yellow gold

Opening act the daffodil
In gardens, parks and window sill

Tickling hearts with gentle thrills
Spring is prepping her bright new frills

A Grand Stretch

There's a grand stretch in the evenings
Darkness is in retreat

Brightness shyly coaching us
Back out onto the street

Pale new light in timidness glows
We wait and watch
As her confidence grows

Week by week she gathers strength
Till day wins victory in its length

Night crawls back into his box
Puts on cap and pulls up socks
Alone in his dark and hidden ways
He dreams of returning darker days
I for sure will miss him not
Happy to see light take his spot

Spring Forward

Spring forward
Fall back
Confuses us every time

Clocks have been altering
Since the year dot
Yet ever there is someone
Who duly forgot

So Spring forward now
Into longer days
And remember
To change your clock
In the right way

Your Favourite Spring Memories

Things

That Happen

In Spring

Rhythms

Year after year we grow used
To a pattern and rhythm of life

Sense of normality comforts
Lowering levels
Of stress and strife

Routines may seem unimportant
Indeed they are anything but

When things happen
As they are meant to
It feels right
Deep down to our gut

Spring Cleaning
(Yeah Right)

Sweep, mop, wipe
Vacuum, shake and dust
Convention will say
Spring cleaning is a must

Get rid of clutter
Sponge down the walls
Shine till windows sparkle
Scrub until you fall

Exhausted into bed
Your hard work plain to see
Or
Just write about it instead
Spring cleaning is not for me

Bikinis

Bikinis in the shops
Just the thing you need

As jeans chafe on the bulge
Expanded by Christmas feed

Itty bitty t-shirts
Skirts that hug your bum

Granny clothes are all that fit
You drive home feeling glum

Slimming clubs start to call your name
Time to face this weighty gain

But first you need some comfort sweet
To soothe your pain with sugary treat

And all because you braved that shop
Next year, safe at home you'll stop

Bigger Is Better

Roses are pink
Yellow too
On Valentine's Day
Only red will do

All can see he loves you
Based on how much he has spent
Does he care enough to starve
Or delay the rent?

Bigger is better
Expensive is best
Pay close attention
To the annual love test

The roses, where did he buy them?
Are they premium and fresh
Not a last minute purchase
On his way home from gym sesh?

The date, how did he plan it?
Did it clearly take much thought?
Does the theme match precisely
With the many gifts he bought?

The gifts, are they expensive?
Do they show he knows you well
Will it fill you with pride
To all your girlfriends tell?

The food. is it your favourite
Had he checked the menu first
Do they serve your preferred beverage
To blissfully sate your thirst

The setting, has it good lighting?
Will it make a video clear?
Does he understand the need
For your fans to see and hear?

How wonderful you are
Perfect is your life
Far removed are you
From loneliness or strife

Followers will watch
Wishing to be you
Loved up by a man
Who knows your value truc

Roses are pink
Yellow and black
Valentine's Day
Is no time to slack

Pancake Tueday

Throw some flour in a bowl
Please don't ask "how much?"
A pinch of salt and sugar
No need for recipe crutch

Make a dent in the flour
Break eggs and pour them in
So easy peasy to make
Buying pancakes is a sin

Not the serious kind
That might land you in hell
Punishment is but in flavour
Shop bought never taste as well

Now add some milk
Mix and watch it blend
Let it rest in fridge awhile
Fry later and watch tastebuds smile

Paddy's Day

Standing in the rain
Watching the parade
An annual tradition
That time cannot fade

Wearing of the green
Colourful floats go by
A national expression
That keeps spirits high

Kiss me I'm Irish
Or "Póg Mo Thóin" instead
Everyone's Irish today
Likely to have sore head

Looking strangely green
The drink, the drink, the drink
A national pastime
Many pints to sink

Would you believe me
When I say this to you
I'm Irish but do not drink
That is honestly true

Mock Exams

Mock Exams
Sent to focus minds
Time to set distractions aside

Real exams
Rolling fast towards June
Time to grasp it's happening soon

Then you'll pour out years
Fill your papers full

Spill cramming
Mix logic
While memory must not dull

Life exams
Toughest lessons yet

Time comes when
School results you will forget

Easter Sunday, Chocolate Funday

Visitors brought us sweet treats
Which in Lent we could never eat
Mam would save them in a jar
Eastertime seemed so very far

Tall glass tube filling with sweets
Piling higher week after week

Easter eggs on mantlepiece
Were not quite as safe
One night my brother and I
To the sitting room did race

The back of one egg
We much enjoyed
Rushed back to our beds
With spirits buoyed

Discovery of our crime
Was delayed till Easter Sunday
Parents seemed not much annoyed
We'd amused them
On Chocolate Funday

Smoked Easter Ham

A well earned rest on the couch
Led me into a sleepy slouch

Deep, deep, I dropped
On cushions propped

Till all too soon abruptly woke
To "Mam, why's the kitchen
Filling with smoke?"

At first I did not understand
My mind still craving sleepy-land

Then "oh no, the ham" I cried
Mind no longer sleepily tired

Stumbled to the kitchen fast
Intent on saving our repast

When crispy edges shaved away
We saved the meat of the day

What a clever cook I am
I now know how to smoke a ham

Are You Going Anywhere Nice?

Are you going anywhere nice?
Never mind the price

Spring has sprung
Holiday ads have begun

You will see them everywhere
Whispering to your wish
To escape dull daily care

Book early
Special offers
Bag a bargain low cost

Daydreams drift down desert dunes
Far from the bite of frost

Are you going anywhere nice?
Great deals going on flights

Spring has sprung
Holiday ads have begun

Sometimes staycations must do
Yet these ads
Build a magical fantasy for you

Are you going anywhere sunny
Best way to spend your money

Early bird taking a leap
Pausing not to ask how

Future you can work and pay
Feels so right to book it now

What Rhythms & Patterns Do You Value Most?

Love,
Romantic
&
Familial

Love Nourishes

Love
In its many sizes
Multiple guises
Brings painful shocks
And glorious sweet surprises

Love
Protects us from our greed
Loss brings painful bleed
Hide though we may
Love's nourishment
We ever need

Stretch Marks

When baby first arrived
She drew stretch marks on my heart
Pink and tiny bundle
Brought to us a fresh new start

When baby first came home
Her clothes dried on the landing
Pink and tiny signs
Of a family expanding

When baby settled in
Her every move we studied
Fascinated by this child
Whose glow could not be muddied

When baby called the shots
We would joyfully obey
Tending to her needs
Without question or delay

When baby woke at night
We would groan from lack of sleep
Yet through exhaustion's fog
We would still our promise keep

When baby captured us
She transformed our every dream
Considering her best life
Became part of plan or scheme

Now the line holds jerseys
Pegged up next to jeans
Washing her own clothes
Dreaming her own dreams

Those stretch marks on my heart
Will never fade away
This life of ever letting go
Is best lived day by day

Love, According To Bea

My friend
In love
Her face alight

The early days when fresh delight
Shows up for every call or date
And too long is the dragging wait
Till lovers meet again

My friend
Who knows
That I am there

To listen well and ever care
Show up in love yet set her free
As she has often done for me
Friends through high and low

My friend
Who knew me well enough
To see this time it would be tough

Her love though new
Was growing strong

We'd learned the Bible
Says that's wrong
Her lovers name was Bea

And Bea
She found it odd
This talk of God

She had not marinaded
In the juices of scripture
As my friend or I had done

She'd travelled longer on a journey
We had just begun

And me
Mind fumbled
Structure crumbled

Liberal had been a word
To speak of faith untrue
Declaring truth as suited you

So began my search
For understanding right and true

A view of love too narrow
I slowly laid to rest

When scrutinised
These ancient ways
Could not pass love's test

By the grace of God
Whoever God may be

I breathed a sigh and now could see
The beauty of love according to Bea

What Are Your Thoughts
& Beliefs About Love?

Loss
Comes
In Many Ways

Loss

Loss never fully goes away

Instead we learn to greet it
day by day

Carrying it with us
As we laugh, work or play

Its heaviness may vary
But far
It will not stray

Her Name

Why do people fight off pain
Every time I say her name

Why such need to cheer me up
As if I were a child in sulk

Why convince me she's now free
As if that's truth I cannot see

Yes, yes indeed, I held on tight
Wished her well with all my might
Was that because I loved her so
Or needed her love
I don't know

I do know she was always there
From baby steps to brushing hair
Loving me and my kids too
A mother's heart
Loyal and true

So even if it flickers pain
Do not protect me from her name

Her Last Mother's Day

Her voice no longer
Sounded like her own

Medication mixed with pain
Had changed how she
Would say my name

Her eyes no longer
Danced with mischief bright

Treatments meant to heal and save
Had robbed from her
Though hope they gave

Mam wanted new pyjamas
Could not find a pair of choice
Till she got a recommendation
Then phoned me
In her strange Mam voice

Wanted them for Mother's Day
Seemed pleased when I brought them in
My sister-in-law
Served a thoughtful cake
Mam did her best to grin

Weeks later we said
Our last good-byes
To her voice, her smile, her care

Mother's Day came around again
But Mam was no longer there

What Loss Do You Carry With You?

Only A Bunny

We lost three bunnies last year
Whispered good-bye
To each cutie dear
The first was a shock
Healthy one day
Gone the next

Had hidden himself
As if sensed he would die
Only a bunny
Yet our eyes leaked to cry

Second was jarring
Out of the blue
Attacked

A violent clash
Though vets tried, she still died
Only a bunny
Yet our hearts sorely cried

By the third we were raw
Wearily warn
Resigned

Another farewell
Good byeing without end
Only a bunny
Or family and friend

We lost three bunnies last year
Each one different
Each one dear

Have You Lost A Dear Pet Too?

Your Thoughts About Loss

_____

_____

_____

_____

_____

_____

_____

_____

_____

_____

_____

_____

_____

_____

_____

_____

_____

Family

&

Friends

Family & Friends

They make us laugh and cry
They help us to belong

They joke with us
(Or smoke with us)
Scaling harmonies in life's song

From Avril To April

My daughter was born

On New Year's Eve

Folk often find it hard to believe

When they hear her name

Is April

My daughter was born

On New Year's Eve

She's even been asked

When she was conceived

All because her name

Is April

My daughter was born

December thirty first

Yet April Fools' Day

Has often proved the worst

Hearing the same joke

For a millionth time

Wondering whether to curse or smile

Let me take you back
To when I was a child
Visiting with a school
Friend of mine
(My age was eight
Or maybe nine)

My pal was called Avril
She was proud to explain
How a calendar month
Was the same as her name

This was exciting
Big news to digest
I was intrigued
And suitably impressed

From Avril to April
When changed into English
The name I loved
Both fresh and distinguished

There and then I would decide
How to name a female child

My daughter was born
On New Year's Eve
All those years later
I would still believe

Her name it must
Be April

Comfortable Friends

Comfortable friends

Worn

Baggy fit

Keeping us warm

Covered

They who match

With anything we say or do

Comfortable friends

Laugh or ugly cry

One size fits all

Stretching to shape we are

Not size we hope or wish to be

In low key

High value way

They compliment

Have their say

Comfortable friends

Everyone needs some

In their wardrobe

Shit Shit Shit

Beginning with sh and ending with it

When I think of Granny

This word seems to fit

She would repeat and say it three times

Heard her so often it stuck in my mind

She had her set way

Granny's views could be strong

Yet such was her welcome

She helped us belong

You could call unannounced

Bringing a friend

Granny put on the kettle

All shyness would end

Tea in a cup

Not a big mug

Sugar of course

And milk in a jug

When we were children
Her pond drew us in
Teeming with gold fish
Too shallow to swim

But that did not stop us
From making a splash
With clothes dry and clean
To the pond we would dash

Beginning with sh
And ending with it
When I think of Granny
This word seems to fit

And if I could ask her
If this poem is a hit
My guess is she'd answer me

"Ah shit shit shit"

Crafting Friends

My craft room hidden
Under bead, scrap, flower
In need of quick tidy
Before morning shower

Tidied yesterday's papers
Glues, cutting mat
So busily sorting
Forgot about tap

Kettle filling for morning cup
Became fountain spilling
Must then be cleaned up

Water flowing onto kitchen floor
Splashed from the sink
With voluminous pour

Friends on their way
I'm busy with mop
By now I had planned
To be at the shop

Cake or biscuits
Must be gluten free
To serve to my pals
With coffee or tea

Opened the door
Still in dressing gown
This made them smile
No hint of a frown

Brought their own biscuits
Thoughtful indeed
They were happy to chill
No need for speed

They each created
With style and flare
Made it look easy
Yet finished with care

Laughed till our sides hurt
Serious fun
Craft brings together
The old and the young

Rugby Girl

Mouthguards are not pretty
These boots are not the sexy kind
Rain has ruined your make-up

Girl, this is not the look
Hunky guys have in mind

Rucks don't smell of roses
Scrumming spoiled
your fresh sprayed tan
Mud has streaked your fair face
Girl, this is not the way
To find yourself a man

Mouthguards might protect you
From spouting your old school tosh
Sport has given me focus

Lady, I'm not trying
To be genteel or posh

There is more to my life
Than the stale gender trap
Of living to impress
A fine handsome chap

What Memories Have Been Brought Back To You?

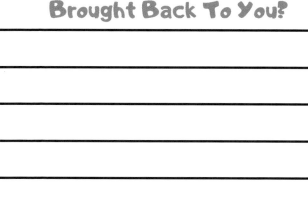

Agnostic
Easter

Agnostic

My faith has fallen apart

Bringing freedom
Served with loss

My sureness days I miss

Not now knowing
What to think

About the Cross

Agnostic Easter

I write this on Good Friday
Sitting in a garden splashed with sun

Our bunny hops then stretches
Beneath the shade of hedges

An ant explores a lonely rose
Counting the days
Till her flower bud grows

Clothes on washing line
Rustle in a breeze I cannot see
Does this garden understand
In ways unknown to me?

I miss the certainties
My faith of old
That life and it's living
Has bashed to unfold

For now I can but look and wonder
Take my time and deeply ponder

Indeed my mind
Cannot grasp
The height the depth
The why the how

So I have been thought
It would befit me more to bow

As sky above
Below us land or sea
Display God's glorious presence
Leaving no excuse
For faithlessness in me

Rocks will cry out
So be wary of doubt

The truth demands
I bend my knee
The majesty of God
I'm told is plain to see

I was schooled to accept
He alone is right
In glory, splendour, Holy might

The Way, The Truth
The One who saves

Who gives pure purpose
To life's short days

No one can come
To the Father
In any other way

Or so for years
Nay decades
I learned to surely say

Now my words are
Maybe, perhaps
Impossible to know

And how oh how
Could a God behave so?

I can quote
Biblical answers
But my heart screams "No"

Where oh where
Did my deep belief go?

My faith was melted
By the heat of diversity

Tumbled by the torrent
Of inclusivity

Scattered to the places
Where unanswered questions go

Leaving me with hands full
Of fluorescent "I dont know"

There are folk
Who know there is no God

There are others
Who know God is Lord indeed

More real than reality
Not subject to anyman's creed

While they who shake
Their heads in disbelief

Appreciate with sadness or relief

Their escape from need
To believe or bow

Giving their best
To life here and now

I write this on Good Friday
Unsettled by the loss
Of things I used to know

Bereaved of belonging
To a God
  a Church
  a Bible
A faith I could turn to
Where direction would prayerfully show

I yearn to believe in God
But not at any cost
Repulsed by the categories
Saved or lost

For this agnostic Easter

What will my basket show?

Chocolate stacked
Amidst whys and hows

And a glaring
Fluorescent

 I don't know

Your Thoughts

Instagram
Poems

Insta Poetry

Some say it's not really poetry
Others think it's the best

Here are some for you
To put right to the test

Monday grey
Or bright fresh start
Interpretation
depends on you
Measures weariness
of your heart
Sandra Matthews

Fell the other day
Nothing broken
Hairline fracture
to the notions of immortality
that hide
where the mind
smuggles in delusion
Invincibility is illusion
Vulnerability is fact

Sandra Matthews

Sublime in storm or breeze
Hills care not who they please
They meditate on now
Inviting us to bow
Low till worries fall into ease

Enough
A word that teaches me
I have enough
I am enough
Tough lesson is to feel enough

Sandra Matthews

Dive head first
Or toe by tippy toe
Fear I cannot shake
Image will not go
Shark in deep end
Of land locked
swimming pool
Waits till I relax
Ponders his attack
Makes of me a fool

Sandra Matthews

Matthews_sandra_ireland_

Author's Note

Thank you again for reading my poetry.

This is the second book in a four part series called "Silly & Serious Seasonal Poetry".
The remaining two will be published over the next year or so.
The first is already available and is called "Winter Warmers Silly & Serious".

A book containing a mix of my old and new poetry is also available. It is called "Ulysses Probably Above My Head".

Take good care.
On with the writing I go.

Love Sandra

My poems are inspired by real life.
With that in mind
I'd like to introduce you to my family.

The human folk would disown me
if I mentioned them here.

So let me introduce you
to my furry family....

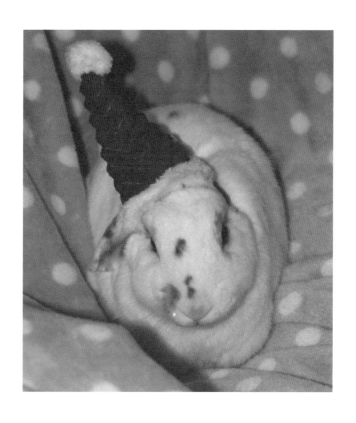

One of our bunnies
wearing her hat.
Her name is Rhea.
Rhea joined our family
when we rehomed her last summer.
She loves her cuddles.

This is our other bunny,
Attis.
He and Rhea are great friends.
A.K.A. Mr & Mrs Bunny.
Attis came to us from D.S.P.C.A.
He finds mischief
everywhere he looks.

Our newest additions
the Guinea Pigs
Rick & Morty

Our Three Dogs

They sleep on our
beds

Nap on our sofas

& even come
on holiday
with us

Our three boys
Draco, Dobby, Snape.
They have formed their very own
neighbourhood watch committee.

Dobby,
the first of our many pets.
He is the leader of the pack
and the most emotionally intune of our dogs.
When we brought Dobby home he was a tiny puppy.
Little did we know that within
a few years we would go
from one pet to seven.

Our second dog,
soaking up some Spring sunshine.
His name is Snape.
Snape came to us from
Dogs In Distress.
He is my little shadow.

Our third dog,
sneaking up on a chocolate stash
when he thinks no one is looking.
His name is Draco, and he really hates
that dogs can't eat chocolate.
Draco is another
Dogs In Distress dog.
He is a loveable rascal.

Pets, Are They Family To You?

Notes

Notes

Notes

Printed in Great Britain
by Amazon